AF489565

BONE HEALTH

BONE HEALTH

STOP OSTEOPOROSIS
PREVENTION AND RECOVERY

A DAILY 15 MINUTES'
SIMPLE ROUTINE

Translation by Lisa Martínez

Enriqueta Martínez Weiss

To all my teachers and students,
who generously shared their wisdom with me.

To everyone that cares about their physical wellbeing,
wishing them a plentiful life.

I travelled round the world following dreams and seeking adventures and surprises.

Whilst climbing a mountain, I met a wise old couple that stood upright and firmly on the ground, munching on an apple.

—Look after your house!

They shouted at me.

— I don't have a house.

I answered.

—You do have one, you're carrying it around! It's your body, the only thing you truly own.

Keep it clean, active, healthy, strong. Nourish it so it can function well. Fill it with love for yourself and the life around you. Look after your body, which is your little house, look after the earth, which is your big house, and lastly look after the universe, which is the biggest house you own!

Index

Please be warned that this publication cannot in any way re-place medical advice.

PREFACE

These days we find an increasing number of people experiencing physical suffering, unable to lead a full life, unable to enjoy freedom of movement or a healthy body.

Bone deterioration and weakness, i.e. osteoporosis, affects a large part of the world's population. In poor countries it is generally caused by a deficient diet. In rich countries, a sedentary lifestyle, processed and unhealthy foods, bad habits and por mental health are in great measure responsible for this condition.

Prevention is the best resource to achieve physical wellbeing and to keep bones healthy. Ideally, we would aim to look after our body from childhood; provided living conditions are not too adverse, we should have the bare minimum required in order to achieve it. Even when damage and deterioration have set, there is always a chance to revert certain symptoms and avoid further harm.

Are we normally taught how to look after our body using our own, basic resources? Are we clearly informed about the benefits of caring for our health and the potential outcome if we don't do it?

Throughout my life and professional career, I have been compelled to follow those basic tenets that guarantee our health and wellbeing. Despite the complexity of our organism and its biological needs, these tenets are easy to understand and follow.
There are five essential functions that us mammals need to guarantee for survival: breathing, feeding, reproducing, moving and excreting. We are gregarious and live in groups in order to help and look after each other; we're highly intelligent and can display evolved behaviours such us respect and tolerance.

How is it that these tenets are neglected systematically in modern society, leading us to disease and lack of wellbeing and freedom? It would seem that some individuals manipulate and distort these tenets in order to blind others and obtain benefits. It iscommon practice nowadays in many societiesfor the powerful to abuse their authority. Hence we continue losing our freedom to care for and respect our bodies and those of our fellow humans, and our ability to solve problems in a natural way; meanwhile big business takes advantage and sells us magic pills to cure what we could have achieved by being free of exploitation and able to look after our health.

Can we look forward to experiencing the daily urge to exercise? Can we look forward to ruling our own lives and choosing not to suffer osteoporosis?

In this book I endeavour to gift you the necessary tools to care for our wellbeing in a self-sufficient fashion, choosing our own in-built and health generating biological mechanisms. Do you aspire to healthy, strong bones, and vitality that lasts into advanced age? I invite you to spring into action!

1

What you need to know
about your bones
and how to look after them

BONE HEALTH

LET CHILDREN PLAY, JUMP,

SHOUT AND LAUGH

LET THEM BE FAMISHED WITH EXHAUSTION

AND EAT TO THEIR HEART'S CONTENT

Bones grow and become stronger during childhood and adolescence.

If bones are adequately mineralised during this time, they will hold a calcium reserve that will be employed when required by the organism in special circumstances such as pregnancy, illness, old age, etc.

In order to keep bones healthy and strong we need a diet rich in calcium and vitamin D, an adequately balanced hormonal system and moderate exercise.

These aspects are often neglected in adulthood due to our hectic lifestyles. We tend to eat badly and are always in a rush and feeling tired. Our pace of life makes it difficult to accommodate exercise and a healthy diet, crucial factors for our bone health. Once we shed responsibilities, as we age, we often find it difficult to change our habits.

A better understanding about bone health will help us be more resourceful when it comes to planning appropriate habits to preserve bones in optimal condition.

Exercise should be incorporated since childhood; during adulthood, when we start losing bone density, we should be particularly aware about the needs of our bones in order to be motivated to look after them.

If you have been unable to look after your diet or exercise throughout your life for any given reason, not all is lost: with simple habit changes we can start to revert deterioration at any stage in our lives.

Our organisms are so generous that if we start offering our body what it needs, it will take it and improve our bone health.

Taking into account the nature of our busy lives, I have devised a range of exercises that can be performed at home. The complete series of exercises takes between ten and fifteen minutes and they are easy to perform – only a small space and a wall to lean on are required.

If performed regularlythey provide a basic training, which will grant you flexibility, strength and agility whilst improving your bone health. They will also increase your physical awareness by providing stimulating new sensations and perceptions that will activate pleasure hormones, which are crucial for our psychic and physical health.

The constant practice of these exercises will guarantee the enjoyment of a healthy and agile body, as well as paving the way for a generally more active lifestyle.

You will be empowered by acquiring a basic knowledge about osteoporosis, an appropriate dietary regime, and the tenets on which the exercise programme is based.

The exercise programme can be self-administered, incorporated into group classes or integrated into different activities.

WHAT IS OSTEOPOROSIS?

Osteoporosis is defined as a state of advanced loss of calcium in the bones, due to which they become porous and fragile.

Your doctor should request a bone density scan to assess the state of your bones; results are usually classified as follows:

Normal – bone density is appropriate for your age.

Osteopenia – bone density is compromised, but less severely than in osteoporosis; it should be a wake-up call to start looking after your diet and to embrace exercise.

Osteoporosis – a significant loss of bone density that requires treatment besides an overhaul in our diet and exercise programme.

Established Osteoporosis – when significant loss of bone density causes a bone fracture.

Bone structure is compromised by demineralisation and weakening, as when vertebrae become squashed.

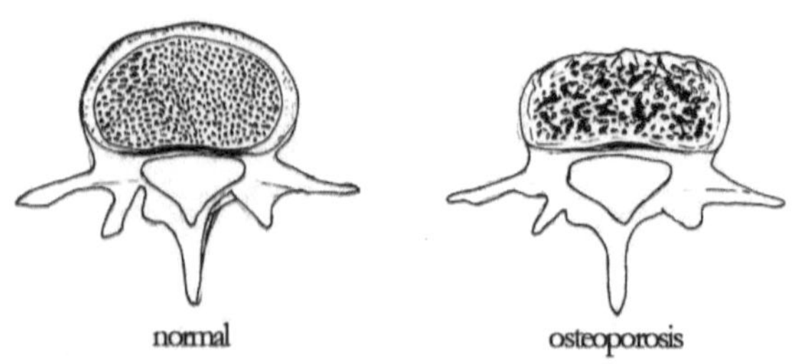

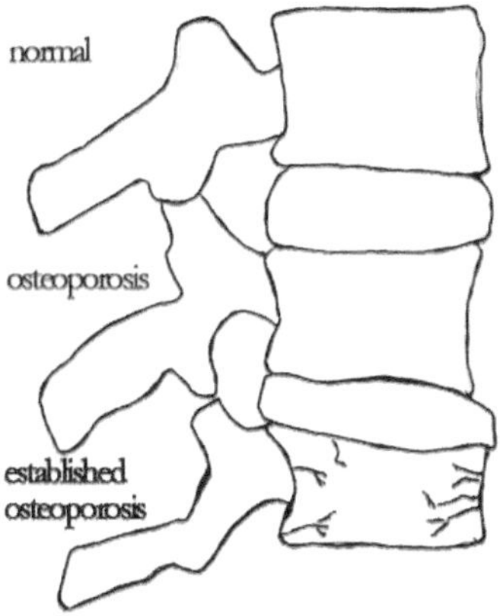

In some cases, osteoporosis affects the external layer of the bone, producing fractures such as the neck of femur fracture, very prevalent in old age.

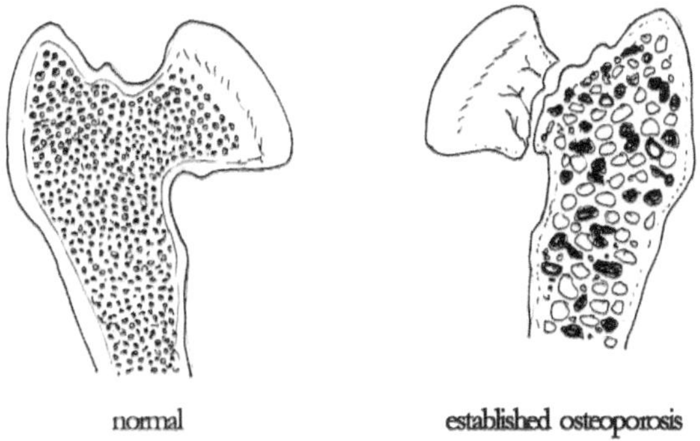

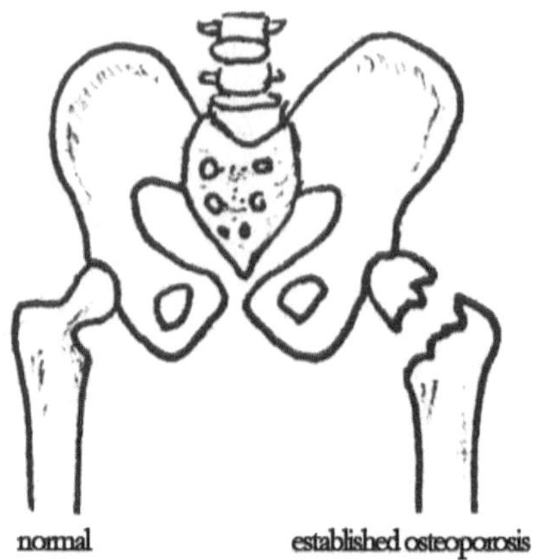

A constant -or prolonged- insufficient calcium intake and a Vitamin D deficit is one of the causes of rickets in childhood and osteoporosis in adulthood.

It is possible that other factors are at play in certain cases of osteoporosis, such as insufficient activation of vitamin D in the kidneys, excessive phosphorous, lack of fluoride or vitamin C, lack or excess of proteins, specific illnesses or hormonal unbalances (e.g. excessive corticoids, alterations in the production of parathyroid hormone, calcitonin deficiency, decreasing sexual hormones, etc.),long periods of immobility or extreme sedentariness.

BONES

As a chemical structure, bones are fundamentally a combination of a protein -collagen-, and a mineral -hydroxyapatite-, composed of calcium, phosphorous and water.

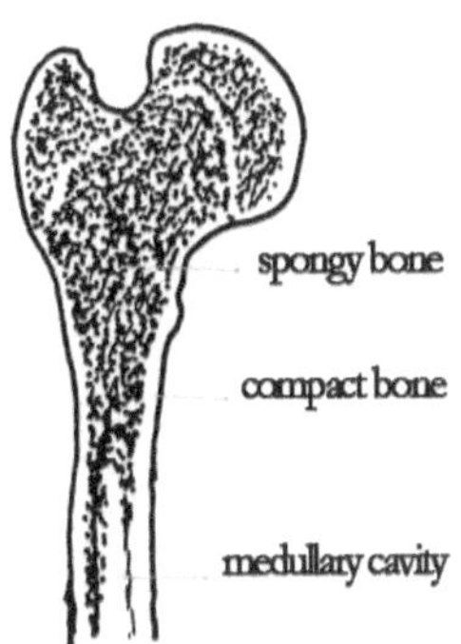

This combination grants bones a level of resistance similar to that of steel, whilst keeping them flexible.
Bones are light, strong and flexible, they can deform and absorb impact without breaking.
The cortical area of the bone is dense and compact, designed to withstandforce.
The internal area is composed of spongy (or cancellous) bone, in the form of plates (lamellae), and is designed to withstand traction, compression and flexion, which in turn are transferred to the compact bone.
The core is taken by the medullary cavity, that transfers forces and increases resistance to flexion. These cavities or canals are filled with red bone marrow and produce blood cells and yellow bone marrow,which stores fat reserves.

Bones are the framework of the body, protect vital organs, fulfil an important role in immunological processes and store minerals -such as calcium and phosphates- which are crucial for essential biological functions like nerve conduction and heart muscle contraction.

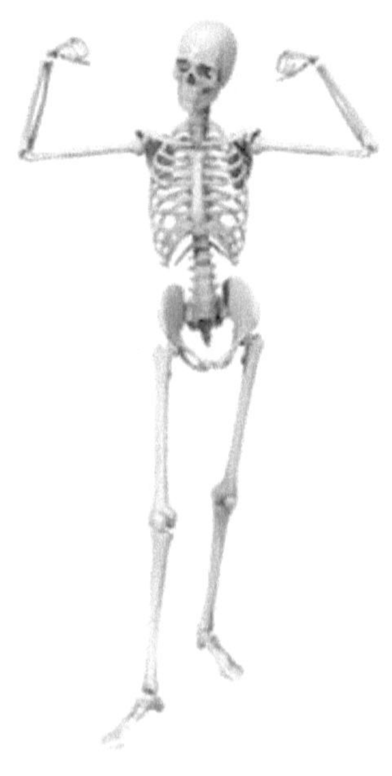

The human skeleton is comprised of between 206 and 240 bones, articulated in a way that determines shape and size of the body; it is designed so that muscles interact with it and generate motion. Our skeletons are continually changing throughout our lives.

Several studies maintain that bone density increases during childhood and adolescence, reaching its maximum peak between 18 and 28 years of age; some studies establish said peak between the ages of 30 and 35. Once this is reached, bone density is lost on an average of 0,3% to 1,0 % per year, both in men and women. During the menopause women lose up to a 3% due to oestrogen deficiency, then reverting to previous percentages. These losses can be reverted by a great deal through appropriate diet and exercis.

During growth spurs, bones change their size and shape through a process named "modelling", a process in which either bone formation or bone resorption occurs on a given bone surface.

If during childhood and adolescence there is good nourishment and physical activity including running and jumping and the body is exposed to sufficient sunlight, bones will develop strength and will have good density.

Once bones stop growing, the "modelling" process continues, replacing bone tissue where it has disappeared, hence eliminating damage and changes in bone structure.

BONES AND DIET

Our food contains a variety of vitamins, minerals and other important nutrients that help us maintain a healthy body.

To keep our bones strong, we need three crucial nutrients: calcium, phosphorous and vitamin D. There are several foodstuffs that provide us with calcium, and it is easier to absorb it in certain groups, as in dairy (70% of absorption).

Calcium (Ca) plays a role in important biological functions suchas nerve impulse transmission, muscular contractility and excitability,heart rate, functioning of cell membranes, permeability of capillary vessels, enzyme activation, and tooth and bone formation.

Calcemia, the amount of calcium present in our blood, has to remain within certain parameters to avoid serious health risks; this is guaranteed by a regulatory system that uses bones as a "central deposit" from which it can withdraw or add calcium as needed, thereby allowing bone tissue to continually reconstitute. For regulation to be successful we need the calcium absorbed by our intestines, the calcium from our bones, vitamin D (which aids calcium absorption from food in the intestines and avoids it being depleted through urination), the parathyroid hormone secreted by the parathyroid gland (which is activated when calcemia is low, recruiting vitamin D and bones' calcium), and calcitonin(secreted by the thyroid gland, increases when calcemia is high thereby blocking the recruitment of calcium in the bones).

Vitamin D is vital in the intestinal absorption of calcium, as without it a great quantity of it would be evacuated through faeces. Most vitamin D is provided by the sun and produced by our body when our skin is exposed directly to it; between 10 and 15 minutes of direct sun exposure three times a week are sufficient, on the face, arms, legs or back, without sun cream. Vitamin D is also present in small quantities in mushrooms, blue fish, dairy and eggs.

The amount of calcium absorbed through food varies between 15% and 60%, depending on specific needs and quantities in our diets. Calcium absorption from food is aided by the presence of lactose (dairy), fructose (fruits), insulin, proteins, vitamin C and some fat. Absorption is diminished with excess of fats (fatty acids increase formation of calcium soaps), and with an overload of sodium, phosphorous, alcohol, sulphates and most importantly, oxalic and phytic acid, which in combination with calcium form salts and insoluble complexes that cannot be absorbed. Nearly all plants contain these acids, to a lesser or greater extent, and if these vegetables contain more calcium than acids, they can be beneficial.If on the contrary they contain more acids than calcium, they could produce demineralisation. Some foodstuffs, like spinach, beetroot, cocoa and tea are rich in oxalates; phytic acid abounds in foodstuffs rich in fibre and in seeds' husks. All of these acids are important for our organism, but in great quantities can impede the absorption of calcium in the intestine.

It is useful to take into account these facts when preparing meals; if there is an excess of these vegetables in our diets, they could produce bone demineralisation. Likewise, if we regularly combine these vegetables with dairy products, we would be preventing calcium absorption from the latter.
The interaction of calcium and phosphorous is vital in our organism, therefore both should be present in similar quantities.

Several studies are consistent in determining calcium daily needs, depending on age and circumstances, on the following parameters:

Babies from
0 to 6 months: 200 mg
6 to 12 months: 260 mg

Children from
1 to 3 years: 700 mg
4 to 8 years: 1,000 mg
9 to 13 years: 1,300 mg

Teenagers from
14 to 18 years: 1,300 mg

Adults from
19 to 30 years: 1,000 mg
31 to 50 years: 1,000 mg
51 to 70 yearsmale: 1,000 mg
51 to 70 years female: 1,200 mg

Over 70 years: 1,200 mg

14 to 18 years, pregnant/breastfeeding: 1,300 mg

19 to 50 years, pregnant/breastfeeding: 1,000 mg

Our diet should be varied and based on local and seasonal fare, which will guarantee that food will be rich in calcium and nutrients.

These are some of the most calcium rich foods:

Approximate measure :
100 g foodstuff per 1 mg calcium.

Dairy products:
Hard cheese 1,100 mg
Soft cheese 400 mg
Fresh, whey, and stretched curd cheeses100 mg

Milk 130 mg
Yogurt 130 mg
Calcium enriched soya milk andrice milk, 80 mg to
200 mg

Animal products:
Rabbit, lamb, beef 16 mg
Egg 60 mg

Seafood 45mg
Poultry 18 mg
Pork 18 mg
Ham (pork and others) 10 mg

Dry or salted fish 3000 mg
Tinned fish 240 mg
Fresh fish 15 mg to 60 mg

Cereals:

Oat 250 mg

Amaranth 153 mg

White bread 151 mg

Bulgur wheat or spelt 110 mg

Wholemeal bread 72 mg

Rye 33 mg

Brown rice 33 mg

Barley 29 mg

White rice 11 mg

Legumes, beans 240 mg

Soy 277 mg

Almonds 216 mg

Lentils,broad beans 60 mg

Hazelnut, sesame 149 mg

Nuts 60 mg

Vegetables:
Turnip leaves 190 mg
Parsley, fresh 138 mg
Beetroot leaves 117 mg

Cabbage 62 mg
Carrot 30 mg
Potato 15 mg
Aubergine, chard, onion, butternut squash, endive, chicory, asparagus, cauliflower, between 20 mg to 60 mg
Red tomato 10 mg

Fruits:
Dried fig 162 mg
Apricot 60 mg
Raisin 50 mg
Orange,mandarin 40 mg
Dried fruits 38 mg
Kiwi 34 mg

Blackberry 29 mg

Lemon 26 mg

Loquat 16 mg

Cherry 16 mg

Coconut pulp 14 mg

Peach 13 mg

Pineapple 13 mg

Mango 12 mg

Hard cheese has a high fat content and salted fish a high sodium content, always consult your doctor if concerned about their consumption.

BONES, GLANDS AND NERVOUS SYSTEM

In order to keep our bones strong, we need a diet that provides the necessary components and an organism that functions adequately and maintains a good bone density.

The nervous system is the great organiser and coordinator of the body's functions. It works to keep us alive, allows us to grow and develop in a myriad way and enables us to be intelligent beings.

Our individual and social behaviour is informed by our nervous system, in charge of organising feelings and ideas that reflect us, other human beings and the planet we inhabit. Results will be very different depending on the constructive or destructive nature of this information. Our hormonal system is also susceptible to this information: we could be inundated with stress hormones that disorganise our organism, or with hormones that promote wellbeing and harmonise it.

If our environment is oppressive, let's try to make an effort to change our ideas and behaviour - starting by caring for our body, which will lead us through a path of freedom and respect for life.

The nervous system in animals is in charge of organising the internal functioning of the organism, by connecting data provided by the external world with our internal information, in turn producing behaviour that enables our survival.

Human species carry from birth their own basic and genetically designed plan for maintaining life; from then onwards it is a matter of nourishment, care and education that will nurture the complex structure of social human beings.

NERVOUS SYSTEM

The nervous system is comprised by the encephalon and the spinal cord.
The encephalon - composed by the brain, the brainstem and the cerebellum- is lodged in the cranium's cavity and protected by it.

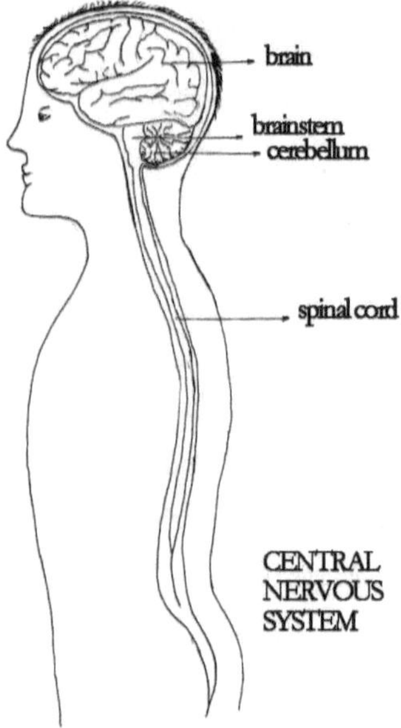

The brain is in charge of receiving, integrating, coordinating and organising the information it receives. It manages basic conducts like hunger, wakefulness, alertness, thirst, sleep, aggression, sexual conducts and emotions. It is also in charge of selecting, elaborating and anticipating behaviours. The most evolved brain region, the cerebral cortex, is responsible for complex functions such as thought, language, creativity etc.

The brain stem is the region that facilitates communication between the brain, the spinal cord and nerves, and controls all vital functions.

The brain controls involuntary movements; the spinal cord, contained within the spinal canal, sends information to the brain and in turn receive orders back which turns into action.

Tasks are shared with regards to fulfilling actions, regardless of whether they are voluntary or involuntary.

Each system has demarcated responsibilities:

The nervous system is in charge of receiving information, integrating it, selecting it, processing it and elaborating responses and complex behaviours.

The autonomic or neurovegetative nervous system organises the functioning of internal organs. It consists of roots, plexus and nerve stems that act as a network of cables that reach organs in order to make them work. Most actions controlled by it are involuntary, such as the sensory and motor innervation of viscera and heart and smooth muscle tissue.

The peripheral nervous system is responsible for our sensations, movement and connection

between the internal and external world. It is made up of an extensive network of nerves and receptors that send information to the central nervous system, where orders and behaviours are programmed.

Those in charge of executing these orders are generally glands and muscles, considered effectors of the peripheral nervous system.

Teamwork is a characteristic of our body, so these systems are interconnected with each other and need each other to achieve a good functioning of the body, and to keep it alive.

The nervous system also organises, regulates and coordinates hormonal function, which plays a very important role in bone health.

HORMONES AND NERVOUS SYSTEM

Hormones are chemical substances secreted by specialised cells such as glands or other tissues. Their function is to act as messengers to provoke specific reactions in our organism.

In the brain -in an area called diencephalon- is the hypothalamus, where emotions (among many behaviours) are managed, and where substances that influence the pituitary are secreted.

DIENCEPHALON

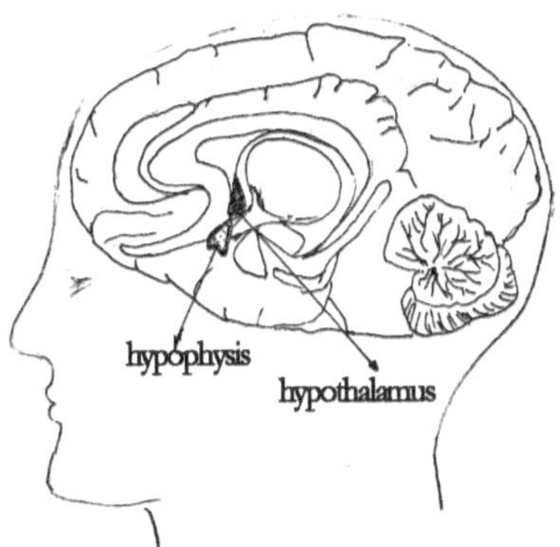

The pituitary is a very complex gland, located at the base of the skull.

The pituitary is responsible for regulating and controlling other glands, such as the parathyroid, thyroid and sexual glands, that produce hormones which are determining factors in the regulation of bone density.

The brain produces its own substances: neurohormones, neurotransmitters, neuromodulators, which are specific to each need - e.g. states of alertness, pleasure, pain, motivation, creativity, motor activity, etc.

As we see, there is interrelation and communication between the nervous system, hormones and behaviours.

If messages of fear, paralysis, tension or irritability are sent through repeated actions, the nervous system and the body will prepare to overcome the real or supposed danger. It will do so by responding with muscle tension and secreting substances that contribute to alertness and stress. If, on the other hand, messages of activity, freedom and desire to live are sent, hormones of well-being and vitality will be activated.

When we are in good spirits, carrying out an activity that is interesting to us, substances are secreted that prompt us to continue with it. We then generate more hormones and substances that mediate that pleasant state. Pleasure is habit-forming, this is why we become addicted to exercise, to dance, to music, all very beneficial dependencies for health. We produce wellbeing hormones, for instance oxytocinwhen we feel tenderness, encephalin to reduce pain, endorphins when we are happy, having fun or enjoying ourselves, serotonin to balance our mood, and so on.

It is possible that the decrease in the production of sexual hormones during the menopause will cause alterations in the regulatory mechanisms. This is because the ovaries no longer respond to the orders of hormones secreted by the pituitary, for ovulation to begin. If the brain misinterprets this situation, it could complicate it by sending negative messages to the body and thus favouring imbalances such as sleep disturbances, fatigue, depression, headache, joint pain, loss of sexual desire, urogenital atrophy, or osteoporosis, all of which often appear to a greater or lesser degree in women who go through menopause.

The hypothalamic thermoregulatory centre may also be unsettled during the menopause, which would explain the loathsome hot flashes that drain the patience and energy of sufferers.

Knowing that behaviours, brain and hormonal activity are interrelated should lead us to reflect on the importance of a healthy lifestyle. I believe that if we adapt our behaviours we can influence other systems and thus mitigate negative effects.

Experiencing our body with pleasure, moving with energy and joy, performing physical and creative activities, developing our intellect, communicating and relating to other people in a positive way, empowering ourselves, are some of the behaviours that promote health and harmony in this period of a woman's life.

Nature designs us to have strong bones until adulthood, then tends to lose interest in our bone health.

As we normally live beyond the age of forty, if we want to do it fully, with health and energy, it is convenient and necessary to take care of our bodies, optimising our quality of life with the contributions that science and various related disciplines offer us.

Messages of pleasure, joy and youthfulness influence the whole body in a positive way, counteracting the ageing process.

All the physical activities that produce pleasure connect us with life and positively influence the body and emotions, activating thoughts and hormones that inform our brain that we are well, young and active, even if we are in reality quite old!

Something similar occurs in our relationship with food. We send ourselves positive messages when we eat, with pleasure, foods that we like (and that we also believe) contribute to our health.

The exploration of different foods, with new flavours and smells, will expand our perception and break our habits, leading us to get rid of prejudices, which generally represent a fear of the unknown.

Eat a variety of foods with pleasure, selecting them with healthy and ecological criteria, with information and intelligence.

Enjoy preparing food in diverse and creative ways, savouring those that can be eaten with little preparation or raw.

Peek into the kitchens of the world.
Surprise yourself with different flavours.
Savour the food, enjoy the aromas.

If we connect with our most intimate feelings, we cannot
deny that the foods that comforted us in childhood have
the taste and smell that we love the most.
This confirms the role of emotions in the act of eating.

As it is important to grow also in this aspect, we shouldstrive to be open to new flavours, textures and smells -which does not prevent us from returning, when we feel like it, to our comforting childhood meals.

BONES AND PHYSICAL ACTIVITY

A team, made up of just over six hundred voluntary muscles, sets in motion the articulated support that makes up the human skeleton.

Skeletal or striated muscle is made up of a soft structure composed of muscle fibres, which has the property of transforming its chemical energy into mechanical energy, i.e. movement. Most muscles are attached to bones by tendons. When muscles are in action, tendons transmit force to the bone.

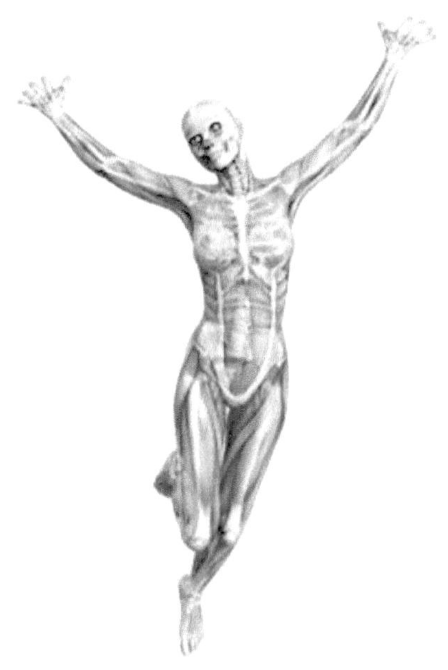

The deep muscles of the skeleton, from head to toe, will contract as necessary to straighten and guide the body to an upright position, thus resisting gravity, i.e. the attraction that earth exerts on objects, bringing them closer to its surface.

From this self-sustained position, the specific muscles that make it possible to run, walk, jump, climb, dance, lift objects -and countless other actions that make us function and give us pleasure, will be put into action.

The forces exerted by the muscles on the bones and the vibrations produced in them by the impact of the feet on the ground, especially when running and jumping, activate signals to increase the uptake of calcium in the bones, thus increasing their density.

Nature is guided by the principle of economy, it strengthens the bones if they intervene in maintaining an erect posture, intrinsic to the human species. If this condition does not occur, there is no point in having strong bones, so they demineralise.

When we have to rest extensively due to an illness, a large amount of bone mass is lost in the first days, which is only recovered when we return to an upright posture and begin to move. Something similar occurs in the case of astronauts traveling to space, where gravity is absent, so they rely on exercise and a special diet to guarantee the least possible loss of minerals in the bones.

The most suitable physical and sport activities for maintaining and increasing bone density are those that exert force on the bones and demand to shift body weight. Impact activities and shaking, accompanied by muscular force, such as walking with some impact, running, jumping or climbing, are beneficial.

These activities are effective even if they are carried out with little or moderate effort, since they require strength to raise the body from its support, and power to carry out the movements.

When we run, head, neck and trunk are raised and pulled forward, stretching the spine. The impact of the feet on the ground generates vibrations in the bones which spread through the legs to the hip and spine, aiding the absorption of necessary minerals in the skeleton.

 Impact activities also positively influence our mood. Movement is part of human nature, indispensable in our lives. It activates the production of hormones and substances that are necessary for the proper functioning of our body and programmes our brains with positive information.

Exercises to prevent osteoporosis and improve bone health require moderate effort and impact: you don't need to get to the point of exhaustion whentraining, it is enough to just feel the heat that produces a feeling of vitality.

Carrying out the exercises with motivation will guarantee that our whole organism, especially our psyche, benefits from them.

It is important to be constant throughout the years in the practice of exercises: the objective is to turn them into a healthy and pleasant necessity. Lack of time and place is not a valid pretext! be it at home, in the park, in the morning or afternoon -only a few minutes are all that is needed.

If we understand the importance of exercise for our health, with only two square meters of space and a modicum of time -ten to fifteen minutes a day- we will give life and dynamism to our body.

Joy and exercise, welcome to our lives!

Embrace activity.

Enjoy your body.

Use the skeletal muscle system with dynamism, adapting effort levels to each stage of life.

ACTIVITIES AND EXERCISES
FOR BONE HEALTH

The best exercises to strengthen the bones are those performed in opposition to terrestrial gravity, in an upright position and in movement.

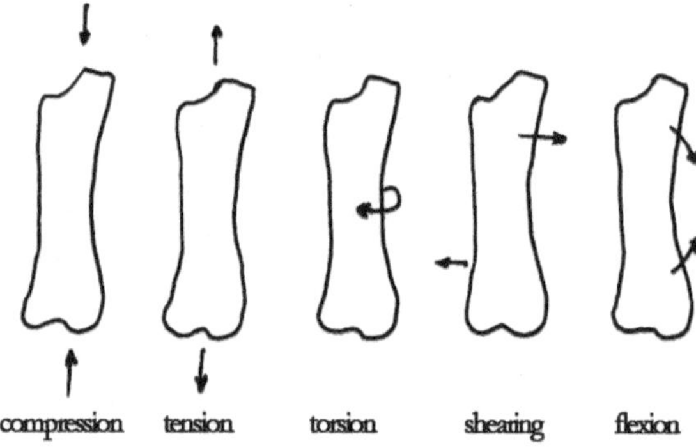

Actions and exercises that combine effort with moderate impact (such as jumping, running, walking with medium impact, hitting a surface, climbing, pushing and lifting weights) exert tensile forces on the bones, shearing, compression, flexion and torsion. Most physical activities combine these forces, which are transmitted to the bones and aid bone mineralisation.

When climbing, all muscles contract towards the target and the grip of feet and hands serves as a fixed point to exert the necessary force.

Climbing is a rich and enjoyable activity at motor level; people who have been able to enjoy it in childhood, climbing trees, will know how stimulating and strengthening this adventure is.

This activity favours psychomotor coordination and generates considerable tensions in different directions which are important for bone health.

Proper distribution of body weight in the axis of gravity, extension of head, spine and supporting muscles are of great help in ensuring good posture.

Dynamic and rhythmic movements that activate large joints promote blood circulation and elasticity, besides generating a feeling of vitality.

In the following chapters we present exercises, organised by specific body movements, necessary to maintain healthy bones.

To see videos of the different exercises please visit **https://www.enriquetamartinezweiss.com** where you will find links to YouTube, organised by page.

2

How do I learn to connect with my
body and
develop more self-esteem?

THREE MINUTES
OF EXERCISES
FOR PERCEPTION AND
BODY AWARENESS

BODY AWARENESS

To have body awareness, we need information from our body. The sense organs are responsible for providing it.

Our sight relays images where we see ourselves as a photograph, as a film.

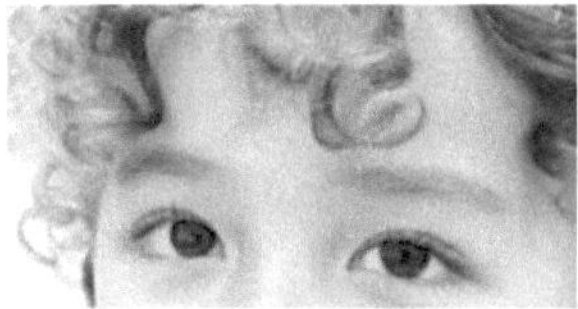

Our hearing allows us to recognise our identity through our voice and sounds.

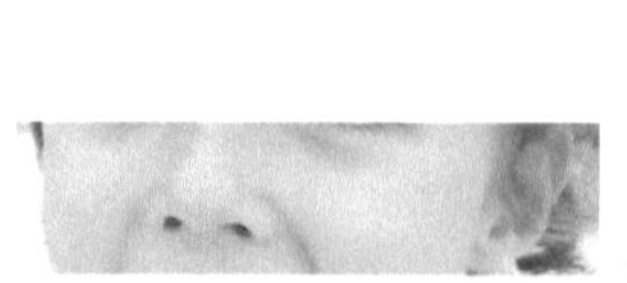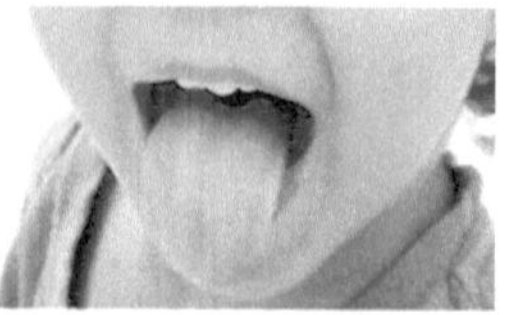

Our sense of smell gives us the gift of identifying ourselves by our unique, individual scent.

Our sense of touch informs us about the surface of our skin, the volume of our body, with its soft and hard parts.

The kinaesthetic sense allows us to feel movement and the possibilities it offers us.

All senses contribute their data so that we have an image, an idea of ourselves.

Our body awareness is constantly changing, the idea that we have of it is continually enriched with the contributions of our senses and our experience.

The exercises in this book will stimulate body perception using all the senses, especially kinaesthetic and tactile. We will carry out activities and exercises associated with pleasure, since learning in pleasant environments is more effective and lasting.

It is useful to have a contact reference with an item. In this case we will use the wall, on which we will support the head, back and pelvis, which will help us to stimulate sensations and perceive the vertical position. We will massage ourselves against the wall, through friction, pressure and light blows to our body. We will pay attention to the texture of our skin, the volume of our muscles, bones, the hard and soft areas, the movement of the joints and the different sensations that will enrich the knowledge of our body and our perception of it.

All this stimulation will generate sensations and a more enriched and pleasant perception of the body, which will give us security and increased self-esteem.

Exercise 1
Shoulder girdle massage

The shoulder girdle is made up of the clavicle and the scapula (shoulder blade). Its joints in the shoulder and the sternum are very important for movement and breathing. Massage will be very beneficial to them.

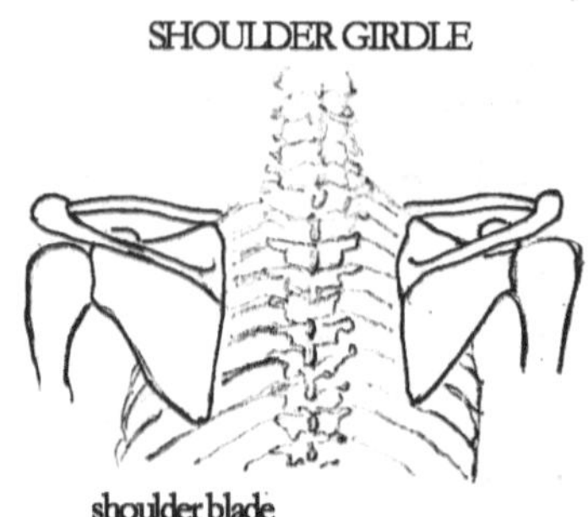

We lean the back of our body against the wall.

We make contact with the hard surface of the wall and feel the areas of the body that rest on it.

We perceive the contact the back of the head makes, the back -especially the shoulder blades area, and hips-especially the sacrum and glutes area.

We stay like this for about three seconds, feeling the position in the vertical axis the body is aligned into.

In both shoulder blades, in the areas of the back that touch the wall, we make slow and gentle rubs, with minimum displacement, drawing small circles and alternating with gentle pressure.

We perform this massage for approximately four to six seconds, seeking pleasant sensations.

We rest for two seconds, leaning our entire back against the wall. During this time our brain will process the experience.

Then, we lean a shoulder blade against the wall and perform the same massage as previously, for eight seconds.

Next, and in the same position, we rest the other shoulder blade on the wall and perform the same massage again, for eight seconds.

During the massage there will be tactile stimulation of the skin and deep sensations. Micro movements will be generated that will give flexibility to the neck and upper chest area, awakening these parts of the body that have been neglected by sedentary life.

We rest for two seconds.

We resume the massage, alternating both shoulder blades, combining friction and pressure.

We aim for our body to be relaxed and free during the massage, so that the effects spread to the deep areas of the shoulder girdle.

We then stop and lean our entire back against the wall.

Focusing on feeling, we let our body and mind relax.

We rest for around five seconds or longer if needed.

We enjoy the relaxation and pleasure from the massage.
We become aware of the body and its sensations.
If the brain registers these experiences without a hurry, it will save them, and the sensations of well-being will be available whenever we want or need them.

Exercise 2
Pelvic waist massage
Glutes and sacrum

The pelvic girdle is made up of the two hip bones attached to the sacrum. It contains vital organs and manages and coordinates movement in all types of locomotion.
Its strength guarantees a full life in old age.

pelvic girdle

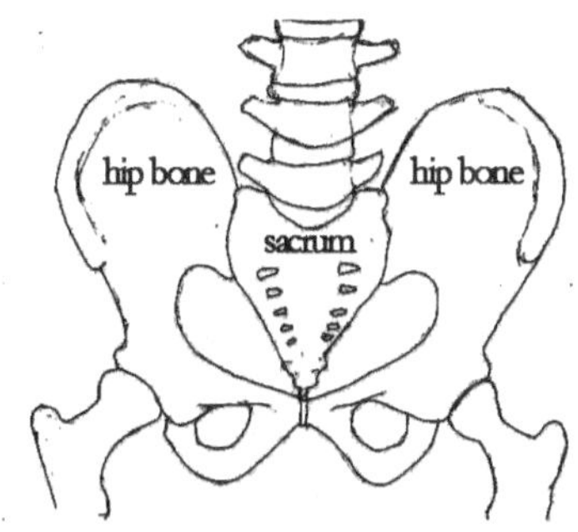

The joints of the pelvis, such as the pubis, the hip joint -
which connects it to the legs- and the joint with the
spine, need to be activated. The correct movement in all
these joints is of utmost importance for health, since it
isresponsible for lubricating and nourishing them, bene-
fitting bones.

The massage that we will perform, both on the bones and on the large muscles that cover them, will generate movements and micro movements that will spread to the small and powerful deep muscles that support the pelvis and permit a good range of movement. These muscles have been forsaken in our sedentary city life. This exercise will prompt them into action.

We focus our attention on the hip. We rest the sacrum bone area against the wall, feeling its presence.

We notice the difference between the soft part of the gluteal muscles and the hardness of the sacrum.

We slide the pelvis on the wall, massaging it with brief circular and lateral movements, with alternating pressure, slowly, for six seconds.

We rest for two seconds.

Then we lean a gluteus on the wall and slide it, with slow friction laterally, and drawing circles with minimum displacement, alternating with gentle pressure.

We continue massaging for eight seconds.

We rest for two seconds.

We repeat the same action with the other gluteus, for eight seconds.

After resting two seconds, we continue with this slow and deep massage, for eight seconds, alternating both glutes.

We rest for two seconds.

We support the sacrum against the wall, noticing the bone, very different from the soft areas of the buttocks.

We repeat the massage alternating glutes and sacrum.

We rest for two seconds.

At the end of the exercise, we lean the head, back, sacrum and glutes on the wall, feeling the areas that make contact with it, and also the presence of those that do not make contact and the spaces that are thus created.

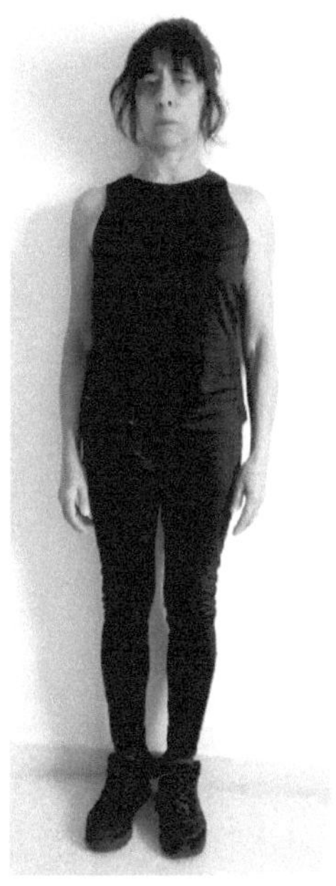

We enjoy the sensations of a stimulated and integrated body, for three seconds. We move away from the wall and become aware of our new presence.

Frequent practice of this exercise will help us perceive and know ourselves better. It will bring vitality, relaxation and well-being to the entire body.

The mind will rest, as it will be focused on the recent sensory stimulation, calm and content.

3

What constitutes good posture?
how to get it?

TWO MINUTES
TO ACTIVATE CORRECT
POSTURE

CORRECT POSTURE

To be aware of our posture we must feel our body and its movement range, its skin, its muscles and bones. At the end of the body awareness exercise, our body is ready to stimulate the muscles that promote a correct posture.

It is the deep muscles, which support the skeleton, that allow us the feat of standing and moving. They are very powerful muscles that exert a great upward force. The strongest are inside the head and initiate any movement that lifts us from restful positions.

Exercise 1
Activate deep muscles
Stretch and raise skeleton

With our backs to the wall, we lean our pelvis on a vertical angle, as well as our shoulder blades and the flat part of the head, which is located in the bony area above the neck.

We become aware of the support and begin a head lift, as if climbing the wall. Our head leads the movement and with its powerful force will pull the neck and back upwards, activating themuscles that support and stretch the spine. The whole body will follow the head on its trajectory.

For this stretch to work, it is necessary that the raising intention resides only in the head.

If the lifting motion is started involving the entire body, a blockage will occur in the deep muscles of the head and neck, which will prevent extension.

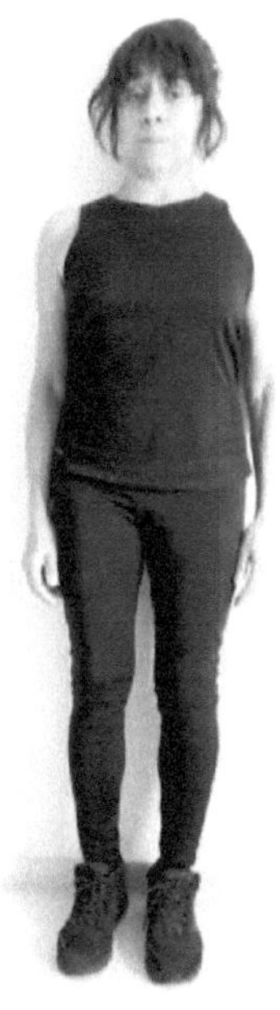

We raise only the head, which will in turn stretch the spine.

We pause in this elevated position for about four seconds, noticing the force employed and the vertical position achieved. Then we relax, without losing the position and intention we achieved.

We repeat the exercise three times, inserting between each of them a brief massage of the shoulder blades and buttocks against the wall.

If someone has a very rigid cervical or lumbar curvature, they should only support the shoulder blades and head, leaving the lumbar area as comfortable as possible; in this way we make a minor, although necessary, stretch of the spine.

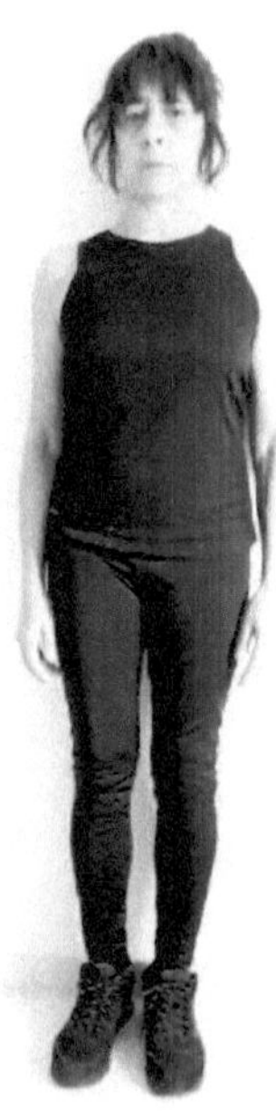

The exercise ends by bringing the rest of the body against the wall to become aware of our newly improved posture.

By performing this exercise daily, you will gradually strengthen supporting muscles and both your passive and active posture will improve.

4

How do I keep my body agile and elastic?

FIVE MINUTES TO ACTIVATE AND INCREASE FLEXIBILITY

DYNAMIC OR AEROBIC EXERCISES

Our body needs movement. Our movement is enacted by the nervous system, muscles, tendons and passively involved ligaments, cartilage and bones. They all work as a team. The nervous system organises the action.

The action may require the muscles to act dynamically, moving the bones at speed, which is what happens when we walk, run, or jump. During these actions muscles work actively, joints continuously adapt to changes in the body's position, and lots of energy and oxygen will be needed, so that our breathing will be deep and fast. This kind of activity gives tone and elasticity to muscle, keeps joints lubricated, increases respiratory capacity, activates blood circulation, stimulates nutrition processes of the skeletal muscle system and produces great energy expenditure.

We will refer to this activity as aerobic.

With these exercises I propose to aerobically activate our musculoskeletal system, especially those muscles we seldom use in our urban lives. I refer to the musculature that intervenes in deep breathing, in the support and mobility of the spinal column, in the functioning of the shoulder girdle and pelvic girdle, and also of the extremities that join them, arms and legs, as they depend on their position and mobility.

It would be ideal to walk, climb, run through fields and parks, but this is not always possible due to personal or environmental barriers, or lack of time.

Since movement is necessary, I would like to propose easy exercises to do at home, such as running on the spot or exerting resistance against a wall.

Activities that demand rapid turns of the shoulder girdle and pelvic girdle -such as those that were once required by fruit harvesting, chopping and gathering firewood- or various rural activities, have now been replaced by machines and are no longer present in today's daily life. Few turning movements are carried out daily, they are small in range and insufficient to mobilise the shoulder girdle.

Our spine and chest are frozen by immobility and gradually stiffen. We end up getting used to it and this deficit, with time, seems natural to us. However, our body cries out for mobility with nervous or listless reactions.

The human body is designed for movement, walking, running, jumping, climbing, picking up, pushing, etc. Unlike other animals, we stood up, the shoulder girdle and the pelvic girdle were placed in an upright position, and we developed a brain and a psyche that asks our body to project itself. To do this we will perform trunk rotation exercises and mobilisation of the ribs, which will partially supplant the movements that climbing requires.

Exercise 1
Respiratory cardiovascular activation
Running on the spot

We will do some mock running, energetic but without advancing. We get ready for action.

Although it is not possible to move, we will put all the effort and energy that moderate running would require.

We will activate the muscles involved in intense breathing, we will feel heat and our heart will pump.

We will generate psychic disposition for exercise.
We are ready to begin.

Standing, in a position ready to run.

We run on the spot, alternately raising the feet off the
ground, about five centimetres; when touching the
ground, we aim to produce a small impact against the
ground.
We free our body to accompany the speed that we generate during this activity.
Our skeleton will shake with each impact and bones will
be subjected to different forces.

These jerks activate internal muscles which hold our internal organs in the right place.

If our footwear is suitable for running and cushions our feet adequately, we can gradually increase the intensity of the impact, over time.

We must however be careful with our feet, as they will need to adapt to new demands. In this way we will avoid fasciae irritations.

If we imagine that we run, the movement of our arms will accompany the legs in a synchronised manner, creating a backward impulse, demanding rib movement and expanding the rib cage as we need more air.

If we increase the intensity and speed of the exercise, the breathing rhythm and heart rate will be higher.
We aim to become agitated and to stay that way for ten to thirty seconds, then gradually we slow down until we stop. It is not advisable to stop running abruptly.
The duration of the exercise depends on the person's age and physical condition. It is advisable to observe our body; if it responds, demands can be increased little by little. In general, between ten and forty seconds are enough -an indicator of achievement is feeling hot and agitated- at which moment it is advisable to sustain this

state for a few seconds and slowly reduce rhythm and intensity until we stop.

The purpose of this exercise is to activate natural mechanisms implicated in running, an activity intrinsic to our species.

Exercise 2
Activation of chest muscles
Trunk rotation with arms across the chest

Standing, legs slightly apart, arms across the chest.

We keep our heads looking straight ahead to avoid getting dizzy.

The hip will remain as still as possible, as it will act as a fixed point for the rotation.

We rotate our trunk, from right to left or vice versa, continuously and with momentum.

We do ten to twenty full rotations in a row, counting the movement on both sides as one.

We must allow breathing to occur freely and naturally, without directing or controlling inspiration or expiration -our body regulate the amount of air it needs. During rotations, we might hear a sound or hiss, which is due to poor flexibility in the ribs and lack of elasticity of the muscles involved in breathing. With daily practice, they will recover the tone and elasticity suitable for their proper functioning and breathing will become harmonious.

With this exercise back muscles will be set in motion, especially those that have an oblique path towards the spinal column and are inserted into it.

We will achieve elasticity and tone trunk muscles. We will increase the rotation scope of the vertebrae and the mobility of the spine.

Trunk rotation with arms crossed at the back
Standing, legs slightly apart.

We look straight ahead to avoid getting dizzy.

The hip will remain as still as possible, as it will act as a fixed point for the rotation.

With our arms crossed at the back, we perform trunk rotations to each side, guided backwards by our shoulders.

We make ten to twenty rotations in a row, (count both sides as one).

Movement should be energetic, rhythmic and continuous, but avoiding jerks.

We must allow breathing to occur freely and naturally, without directing or controlling inspiration or expiration -our body regulates the amount of air it needs.
As in the previous exercise, breathing may become more laboured during rotations, which should not worry us.
This exercise will lend us greater muscle elasticity in the high and lower areas of the ribs and the shoulder girdle, which are especially affected by sedentary life.

Exercise 3
Pelvic and lower limb activation exercises

When climbing trees or mountains our legs need to overcome obstacles and so lower limbs' joints and hips move
in all directions.
I would like to propose exercises to replicate these
movements that our body needs but that are absent in
urban environments.

Leg swing
Standing, body lateral to the wall and with one hand resting on it.

We swing one leg back and forward.

The height of the leg lift will be determined by the strength and elasticity of the muscles.

The movement must be fluid, without forcing the lift, as eventually it will become more efficient.

We do ten to twenty repetitions.

We change orientation of the body, resting the other hand on the wall and repeating the same movement and amount of repetitions with the other leg.

This exercise alternately stretches and contracts the front and posterior muscles of the pelvis and legs, including quadriceps, femoral, psoas, glutes and deep muscles of the pelvis.

Side leg lift

The lateral leg muscles are barely used in our daily urban life. We will activate them with this exercise that will improve elasticity and blood circulation in the hip-leg joint, it is ideal to promote the health of the coxofemoral joint and femur (leg bone that articulates with the hip), which is affected in osteoporosis, usually due to lack of movement.

These leg exercises -forward and back swings and lateral lifts-, increase lubrication and blood circulation in the area, therefore improving nutrition.

Facing the wall, both hands resting on it to help us maintain balance.
Legs together, feet and knees aligned forward.

Raise leg laterally; avoid forcing it beyond the anatomical barrier, keep foot and knee forward.
Return to the starting position.
Repeat the movement fluidly between ten and twenty times in a row.

From the initial position, do the same exercise with the other leg.

If it is tiring, or the leg we're standing on buckles up, we can reduce the number of repetitions on each leg, alternating legs, until the ten or twenty repetitions are completed with each leg.

This exercise helps activate the coxofemoral joint and aids its lubrication and nutrition. We perform a tonic action on the muscles that bring the leg close and then away from the midline of the body, especially the gluteus medium, adductors and thigh abductors.

5

How do I apply resistance
on my bones
to strengthen them?

FIVE MINUTES
OF MUSCLE WORK

LOAD AND STRENGTH TRAINING EXERCISES

In a variety of circumstances, muscles may need to release a lot of energy, such as when running fast, climbing on difficult terrain, jumping with momentum, or lifting, pushing, throwing, or holding heavy objects. During these actions, joints will be properly set, and muscles will recruit many of their fibres into action, increasing in size during contraction.

When we perform actions that require strength, muscles press on the bones and strengthen them.

In activities that require resistance, breathing becomes slow and intense when strength is exerted, and blood concentrates on the muscles that need it the most, until exertion is over and they regain its normalcy.

It's called static contraction muscle work.

To improve tension on the bones, it is necessary to work in an upright position using our body weight distributed on the axis of gravity -the forces thus exerted will be more effective.

strength resistance on the bones will be performed moderately.

It is important for the effectiveness of this activity to perform it, ideally, daily, or at least on alternate days.

We will perform arms' resistance exercises, which will have an effect on the muscles of the chest and spine. We will strengthen pelvic waist and legs' muscles by jumping in different positions - this constitutes one of the most complete exercises for this area of the body. When we jump, the muscles of the head and the spine are activated, alongside a large amount of other muscles, especially abs and glutes.

The forces generated by the jumps are transmitted to the bones, strengthening legs, pelvis and spine, while generating a feeling of vitality.

Legs and arms exercise series will be performed in an alternating fashion. Jumps should be low, between two and ten centimetres from the floor. When resistances are performed, we should be aware that muscles tighten and increase their volume. As a result, body heat will be generated due to exertion.

The number of repetitions will be adapted to the person's age and their physical and health condition. The number of repetitions suggested for exercises are based on the tolerance average. The amount can be increased or decreased depending on level of fitness.

You can repeat the series wholly or partially, several times a day, if you have the time and the motivation for it.

In case of advanced or established osteoporosis, a doctor should be consulted prior to start of programme.

Exercise 1
Strength in trunk and arms (biceps)

We begin the exercise by standing, legs slightly apart, upright body facing the wall.
We rest both hands on the wall, placing them at chest height, with arms slightly bent.

We maintain a separation from the wall, marked by the distance between the supported hands and the slightly bent arms.

In this position, we sustain pressure with our arms and hands against the wall, as if we were pushing it or resisting its fall.
We feel the tension that is generated in our arms and chest. We keep a relaxed face and jaw.

We bring the shoulder blades closer to the spine, towards the center of the back, to increase the strength.

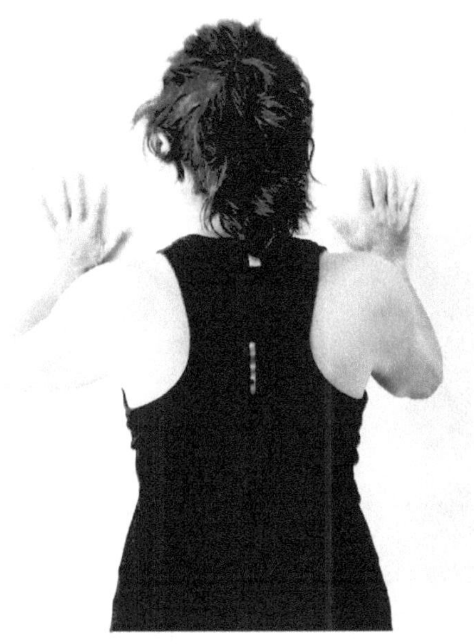

We sustain the effort for three seconds.
We rest for a second from the tension, without lifting our hands from the wall.
We repeat the exercise ten times, resting a second between each repetition.
With these exercises we develop strength in the arms, especially in the biceps and back muscles.
There is a variation to this exercise, it can be performed lifting the hands off the wall, between two and ten

centimetres, then dropping them on the same place, with a moderate impact.

In this case we can do five repetitions simply supporting the hands and five repetitions with separation and support with impact.

These exercises generate vibration and greater tension along the arms and chest bones, hence stimulating their mineralisation.

It is useful to observe and feel how the muscles of the back increase in size and the shoulder blades approach the spine, guided by the muscles that attach them to the skeleton. Arm muscles also build strength and increase their size.

Exercise 2
Close-legs jumps

We will boast our muscular strength, in an upright position and respecting the body's axis of gravity. Generating slight impacts when jumping, we will strengthen muscles of the spine, pelvis and legs.

Upright position, feet together.

Facing the wall, with a separation equal to that marked by the arms in slight flexion.
Hands resting on the wall at chest height.

Lifting the feet from the floor, between two to ten centimetres, perform ten jumps alternating each foot, rhythmically.
These alternate jumps will prepare the body for the next exercise, boast psychomotor coordination, warm up the muscles, and deliver a smooth impact.

Return to the initial position and perform ten jumps with both feet at the same time.

Older people with a sedentary lifestyle could start with a lower number of alternate jumps and gradually increase quantity and difficulty, until completing the entire series.
In the case of osteoporosis sufferers, jumps can be replaced with alternating light blows on the entire sole of each foot against the ground.
As strength, endurance, and confidence are gained, you can advance to the full series.

Exercise 3

Back and arms strength (triceps)

We will develop strength in the back and arms, especially in the triceps muscle.

Standing upright, facing the wall, legs slightly apart.

Arms outstretched, raised above the head, both hands resting on the wall.

 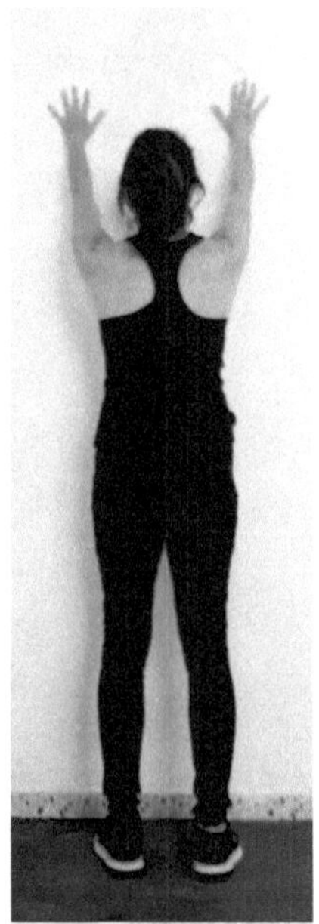

In this position we exert, with arms and hands, a sustained pressure against the wall, as if we were pushing it or as if we were resisting its fall.

The body remains upright as in the initial position. We sustain the pressure for three seconds. We rest a second without lifting hands off the wall.

We repeat the exercise ten times in a row, with a second's rest between each one.

This exercise can be performed with greater force, with the variation of lifting hands off the wall, two to ten centimetres and letting them fall in the same place, exerting a moderate impact as well as resistance.

 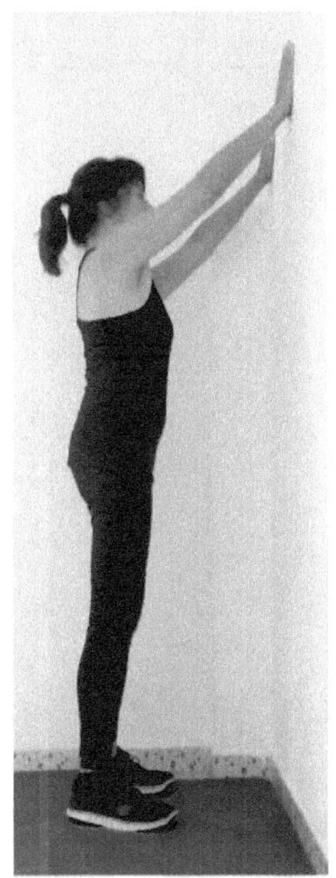

In this case, we can do five repetitions with support and five repetitions with lifting of the hands and support with impact.

Exercise 4

Jumps with legs apart

Jumps on the spot with legs apart require more effort than those with close-legs as impact spreads over a greater area in the pelvic girdle, strengthening bones.

The muscle tension produced to lift the head and trunk increases during jumps, which strengthens muscles and bones.

We stand upright, facing the wall, with a separation that allows us to lean on it if we need to. Feet about hip width apart.

Lifting feet from the floor, between two and ten centimetres, we perform ten jumps alternating feet in a rhythmic way. These alternate jumps improve movement coordination and warm up the body, preparing it for the next exercise.

When finishing alternate jumps, return to the starting position.

We prepare to perform jumps with both legs at once. We perform ten jumps in a row.

Jumps with both legs at once can be incorporated little by little, since they require more effort than the previous exercise.

You can start with five alternate jumps and continue with five simultaneous jumps. As a goal, aim to perform ten alternate jumps and ten simultaneous jumps.

The impact of the feet when falling will be greater than in alternate jumps, it will increase energy expenditure and a sensation of heat that will generate vitality.
Body shakes that occur during jumps serve to better position intestines and other internal organs in their cavities.

Older people with a sedentary lifestyle could start with a lower number of alternate jumps and gradually increase the quantity until reaching a complete series.

Osteoporosis sufferers can start gentle tapping the entire sole of the foot on the ground, alternating each foot. As you gain strength, endurance, and confidence, you can progress to the full series.

In cases of advanced or severe osteoporosis, consult your doctor or physician.

Jumps exert tension on the entire musculature in the body's axis of gravity, strengthen muscles of the spine, pelvis and legs, especially adductors and abductors, and their impact is transmitted in the direction of the greater trochanter of the femur, a bone that is frequently affected in osteoporosis.

Exercise 5
Strength in trunk and arms (deltoids)

With these exercises we aim to create muscle tension and strength in the trunk and rib area, especially in serrated muscles. They will help develop strength in the arms, especially in the deltoid muscle.

We stand in an upright position, sideways from the wall, legs slightly apart. The arm on the side of the wall stretched out, raised to shoulder height, drawing a straight line with it.

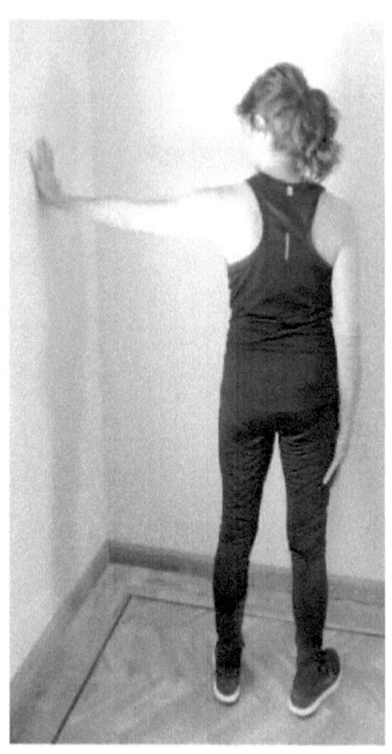

In this position, we exert a sustained pressure against the wall with the arm and hand, as if we were pushing it or as if we were resisting its fall.

The body remains upright as in the initial position. We sustain the pressure for three seconds.

In this way we generate a tension in the arm, especially in the deltoid muscle, which is transmitted to the rib cage.

Rest and relax the tension for a second without lifting the hand resting on the wall.

Repeat the exercise ten times in a row, resting one second between each push.

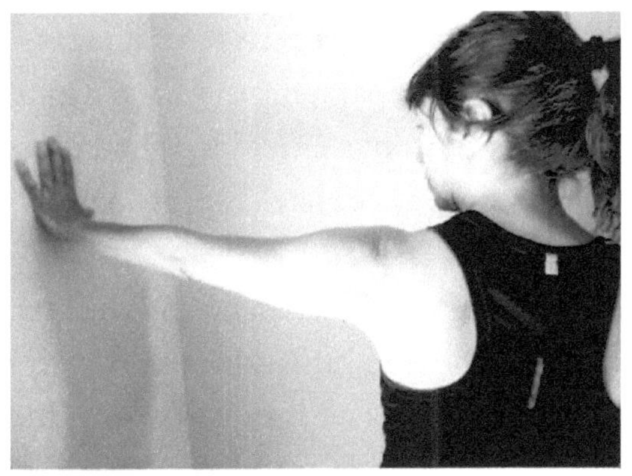

When pressing against the wall, we must prevent the elbow from flexing while tensioning.

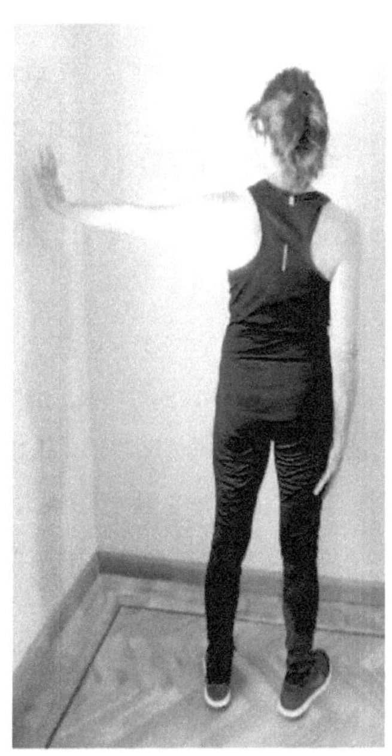 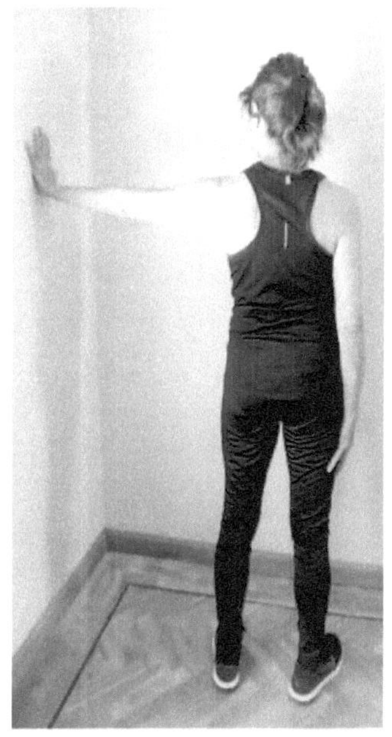

We can perform this same exercise to increase strength, with the variation of separating the hand from the wall, between two and ten centimetres, and then dropping it in the same place, with moderate impact, before we apply resistance.

In this case, we perform five repetitions with support and five repetitions with hand lift and support with impact.

This exercise strengthens and tones the arm muscles, especially the deltoid muscle, shoulder blades, chest, and the muscles in the chest, between the ribs, in charge of expanding them during breathing. The force is transmitted laterally to the shoulder girdle and spine.

Exercise 6
Jumps with lead leg

This exercise requires a bit more effort; it aims to exert tension on the body's axis of gravity, generate impact when jumping in the direction of the pelvic floor, sacrum, lumbar vertebrae and strengthen muscles of the spine, pelvis and legs.

When jumping in this position, the forces are mainly exerted from the quadriceps, hamstrings and buttocks, in the direction of the pubis and the pelvic floor, travelling towards the spinal column and chest, reaching the head.

The vibrations and shocks produced by the jumps spread throughout the body.

We stand upright, facing the wall with
a gap that allows us to lean on it, which

we will do if we consider it necessary.

Legs apart forward and backward.

Feet about hip-width apart. If we start the jumps with the right leg forward, when repeating the series, we invert the position placing the left forward.

Raising the feet from the floor, between two and ten centimetres high, we perform ten jumps alternating both feet in a rhythmic way.

We try to exert a moderate impact when the foot hits the ground, producing vibrations that are beneficial to the bones.

We perform ten jumps in a row, alternating legs.

At the end of the series of jumps with alternate legs, we return to the initial position.

These jumps will strengthen muscles of the spine, abdominals, glutes, pelvis and legs.

Exercise will produce heat and beneficial shaking in the body, which will spread from the pelvis to the chest and reach the head through the spine.

The sensation of heat and the shaking can be uncomfortable and unfamiliar, but let's not be intimidated by it, we should experience them with joy as they are a sign of vitality.

We return to the initial position, distributing the weight of the body in the axis of gravity. We rest for two seconds.

From our initial position we perform ten jumps with both legs at once. We rest while we change the position of the legs and repeat the series of jumps.

Jumps with both legs in this position require more effort than alternate jumps, so the energy expenditure will increase, the sensation of heat will be greater, and the breathing will become more intense.

Muscles will increase their force and tension on the bones, improving bone density.

6

How can I feel fulfilled?

FIVE MINUTES OF WELLBEING AND CREATIVITY

ENJOYING OUR BODY
ANDPOSSIBILITIES OF MOVEMENT

It is important to consider the body as a whole and to work, even if briefly, on all its aspects.

Our body seeks harmony and cadence in movements. We aim to release our body through free and creative movement.

The human body can make large lever movements, such as push-ups and knee, elbow, shoulder and pelvis extensions. We made some of these movements in previous exercises.

Other, less spectacular movements are nevertheless very necessary for our physical and mental health: those of small joints such as between the sternum and ribs, inter vertebrae joints, between vertebrae and ribs, hip joint and legs and pelvic floor joints.

These complex joints are activated by small and powerful muscles, capable of both supporting and giving flexibility and movement to structures in charge of vital functions such as breathing, excretion, sexuality, etc.

These movements are crucial as they help regulate vital functions and awaken sensations and emotions rooted in survival.

I would like to propose a simple and enriching exercise that activates these joints and muscles gradually, with easy and pleasant movements.

If we stand upright in the centre -or in any available space- of the room we're in and observe it, we see that it generally has angles in the corners of the ceiling and floor.

The task is to bring both shoulders and hips in the direction of those angles and corners, thus generating movements in these joints.

Shoulder girdle movements

We stand in the centre of the room we are in. We choose a corner of the room and focusing on one shoulder, we direct it towards it.

We direct our shoulder, with small movements, towards the chosen site; in this way, the shoulder girdle and ribs also move in that direction, dragging the rest of the body with it.

Once we have explored how far we can go with our shoulder, we change direction, choosing another angle of the room.

The shoulder moves slowly, projecting, exploring up, down, back, forward, looking for opposite angles.

We can work with a single shoulder first, discovering the different projections, or we can explore a projection with one shoulder and then with the other.

The head and spine will also be stretched, following the shoulder's direction. In addition to freeing our range of movement, we perform a deep muscle stretching and flexibility exercise.

If we let ourselves be guided by the intention, movement will occur smoothly and effortlessly.

We aim to spend a minimum of two to three minutes enjoying this easy and rewarding exercise.

These movements will encourage proprioception, generating wellbeing, stimulating pleasure hormones. We will feel that our body is full of life and that it responds to our will to move, generating self-esteem.

Pelvic girdle movements

We will use the same strategy as in the previous exercise to mobilise the pelvic girdle. We will project with small movements, one hip first and then the other, towards the different angles of the room.

We direct the hip towards an angle of the room, relax a moment and move again demanding a little more each time, so muscles will gradually give way, effortlessly, in a game of relaxation and tension.

We change direction with the same hip and perform the same projection game. We explore a minimum of four directions towards angles in the room. This will put into action the deep musculature of the pelvic floor and the junction of the hip with the spinal column.

We perform the same movements and similar projections with the other hip, focusing specifically on the iliac crests, the pubis, the sacrum, and the hip-leg joint. We focus our awareness in these areas and project them in different directions.

We feel how the muscles are activated and how these in turn generate new small and intense movements; we focus on enjoying them and letting ourselves be carried away by pleasure and exploration.

Integrating movements

Once the shoulder girdle and pelvic girdle are released, we are ready to enjoy and coordinate the movements of both.

We now project randomly to different angles of the room, shoulders alternating with hips, replicating our previous motion and enjoying the pleasure of free movement.

We will be pleasantly surprised by the vast possibilities that our body has of generating its own dance.

Once we have captured a true experience of pleasant physical liberation, we can add music to this event.

Enjoy! Pleasure and movement will be in charge of generating health.

Summary

Smart recap of the

**FIFTEEN MINUTES
SERIES OF SIMPLE EXERCISES**

"BONE HEALTH"
stop osteoporosis
prevention and recovery

To see filmed demonstrations of the exercises
in YouTube ordered by pages, please visit:
https://luciameltec.wordpress.com
YouTube: maria martinez weiss
YouTube: luciameltec

THREE MINUTES
PERCEPTION AND
BODY AWARENESS EXERCISES

Feel your body against the wall.

Self-massage on the shoulder girdle: shoulder blades.

Self-massage on the pelvic girdle: glutes and sacrum.

Integrate both massages.
Perceive and feel the entire body.

TWO MINUTES
TO ACTIVATE CORRECT POSTURE

Back and head supported on the wall.
Raise your head.
Exercise awareness.

FIVE MINUTES
TO ACTIVATE THE BODY AND INCREASE

FLEXIBILITY

Run on the spot.

Trunk rotation, arms crossed on the chest.
Trunk rotation, arms crossed at the back.

Leg swing.
Lateral leg raise.

FIVE MINUTES
MUSCLE STRENGTH EXERCISES

In front of the wall, arms flexed, hands resting on the wall at chest height, exert resistance.

Legs together, alternate and simultaneous jumps.

Facing the wall, arms outstretched and raised, hands leaning against the wall, exert resistance.

Legs apart, alternate and simultaneous jumps.

Lateral to the wall, arm stretched at shoulder height, hand resting on the wall, exert resistance.

Legs spread apart, one forward and the other behind, alternate and simultaneous jumps.

FIVE MINUTES
OF WELLBEING AND CREATIVITY

Mobilise shoulders.
Mobilise hips.
Integrate both movements.

About the author

Enriqueta Martínez Weiss has extensive training in the field of dance, physical education, body work techniques and neuromotor reeducation. Psychology studies and a specialisation in psychomotricity complement her training and inform her concern for body care in all its aspects.

She has taught extensively and worked in the rehabilitation of children, adolescents, adults, and those with motor, neurological, hearing and vision difficulties. Working with women and young people that were victims of abuse or at risk of poverty or social exclusion has reinforced her belief that the body is truly our only asset and we should protect it both on an individual and a social level.

She would like to foster the belief that all genders need to care for, love and enjoy their bodies, which will in turn generate awareness to care for and respect other bodies.

Born in 1945, her education, teacher training and much of her work took place in Argentina. At the age of 40 she emigrated to Spain -where she still resides- and continues to work in various institutions and on a private level.

Currently she spends her time researching, publishing books and educational resources, teaching courses and seminars.

https://www.luciameltec.wordpress.com

Bibliography

ALFONSO M., CALLEJA A. et al. (2002). University Clinic of Navarre *Osteoporosis. Improve the health of your bones.* [h] Publisher Everest. Leon

CASTELO-BRANCO HAYA PALAZUELOS, CJ (2004). *Osteoporosis and menopause.*Panamericana Medical Publishing House, Madrid

LÓPEZ CHICHARRO, J. (2014).*Physical activity applied to osteoporosis.* Elsevier, Spain

GARCÍA ROLLAN, M. (1990). *Human nutrition, mistakes and their consequences.* Mundi-Prensa Madrid

PALACIOS GIL CASTAÑO, S. (2009). *Understanding osteoporosis.* Editorial Amat, Navarra

MAYES, K. (2010). *Osteoporosis, how to relieve symptoms and live a better life.*Oniro editions

Ministry of health and social and equality policies. (2010). *Clinical practical guide on osteoporosis and prevention of fragility fractures.*

XHAEDEZ, Y. (2012). *Vademecum of physiotherapy and functional reeducation.* El Ateneo

COMPSTON, J. (2000). *Osteoporosis.* Editions B. Barcelona.

HERRERA RODRIGUEZ, A. (2017). *Osteoporosis, the silent epidemic of the 21st century.* Editorial Prensas de la Universidad de Zaragoza

BASSEY, J., DINAN S. (2002). *How to strengthen bones, exercises to prevent osteoporosis and avoid fractures.*Parramón Editions

CASTAÑEDA SUARDÍAZ, JG, MILENA ABRIL, A., RAMOS HERNÁNDEZ, M. (2017). T. *Endocrine physiology in health sciences.* Servicio de publicaciones de la Universidad de la Laguna

CEVALLOS ATIENZA, R. (2016). *Disorders of calcium metabolism.*Formación Alcalá

ASCENCIO PERALTA, C. (2011). *Nutrition Physiology.* Editorial McGraw-Hill Interamericana de España

National Institutes of Health *Calcium and vitamin D: important at all ages.* (2015). National Information Center on Osteoporosis and Bone Diseases, USA

Special Thanks

My heartfelt thanks to Rodolfo Castagnolo for composing the music for chapter 6, "Wellbeing and Creativity"

My most sincere thanks to friends and
relatives, who selflessly contributed
with their knowledge and resources
to the birth of this book.